Opposites

for Kids age 1-3

by Dayna Martin

Text © 2015 Dayna Martin
Design © 2015 Engage Books

All rights reserved. No part of this book may be stored in a retrieval system, reproduced or transmitted in any form or by any other means without written permission from the publisher or a licence from the Canadian Copyright Licensing Agency. Critics and reviewers may quote brief passages in connection with a review or critical article in any media.

Every reasonable effort has been made to contact the copyright holders of all material reproduced in this book.

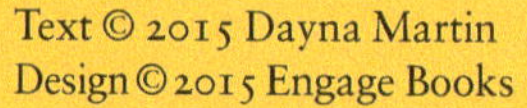

ENGAGE BOOKS

Mailing address
PO BOX 4608
Main Station Terminal
349 West Georgia Street
Vancouver, BC
Canada, V6B 4A1

www.engagebooks.ca

Written & compiled by: Dayna Martin
Edited & designed by: A.R. Roumanis
Photos supplied by: Shutterstock

FIRST EDITION / FIRST PRINTING

LIBRARY AND ARCHIVES CANADA CATALOGUING IN PUBLICATION

Martin, Dayna, 1983–, author
Opposites for kids age 1-3 / written by Dayna Martin ; edited by A.R. Roumanis.

(Engage early readers : children's learning books)
Issued in print and electronic formats.
ISBN 978-1-77226-075-5 (paperback). –
ISBN 978-1-77226-076-2 (bound). –
ISBN 978-1-77226-077-9 (pdf). –
ISBN 978-1-77226-078-6 (epub). –
ISBN 978-1-77226-079-3 (kindle)

1. English language – Synonyms and antonyms – Juvenile literature.
I. Roumanis, A. R., editor
II. Title.

PE1591.M365 2015 J428.1 C2015-903410-8
C2015-903411-6

Opposites

for Kids age 1-3

Engage Early Readers

Children's Learning Books

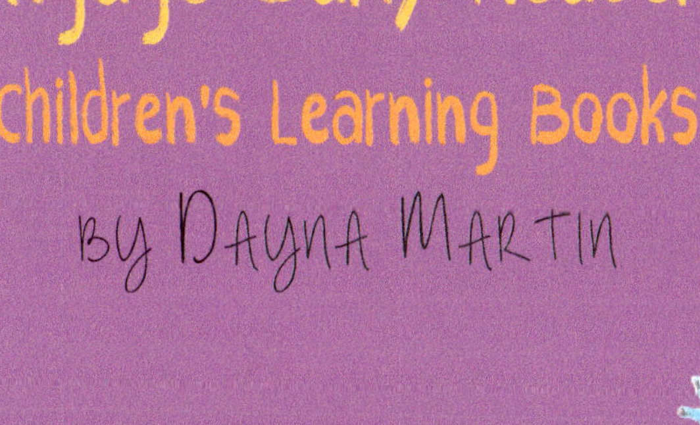

by Dayna Martin

ENGAGE BOOKS / VANCOUVER

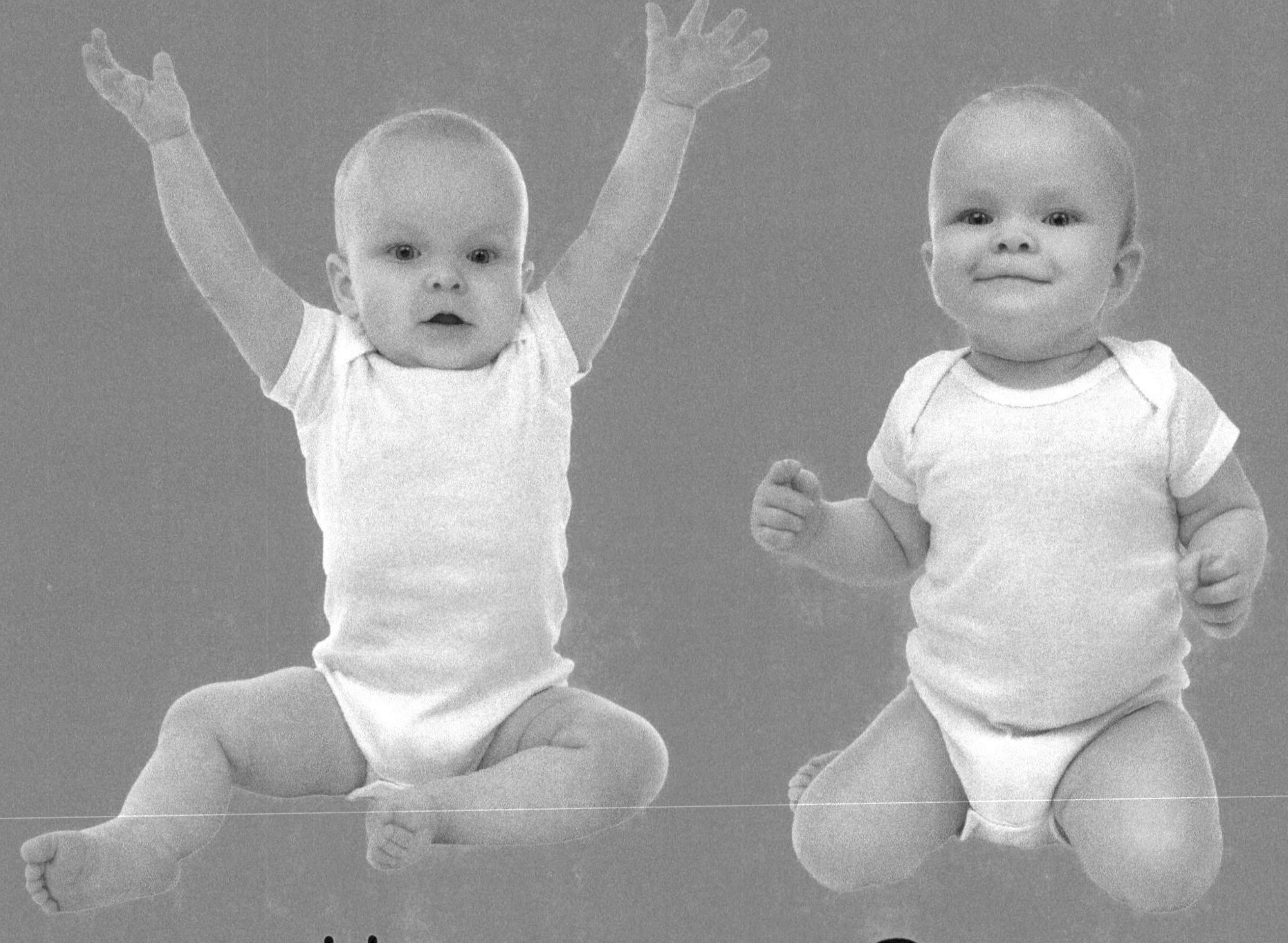

Up Down

In

Out

Big Small

Clean

Dirty

Empty Full

Safe Dangerous

Hot Cold

Wet

Dry

Long

Short

Slow Fast

Few

Many

Front

Back

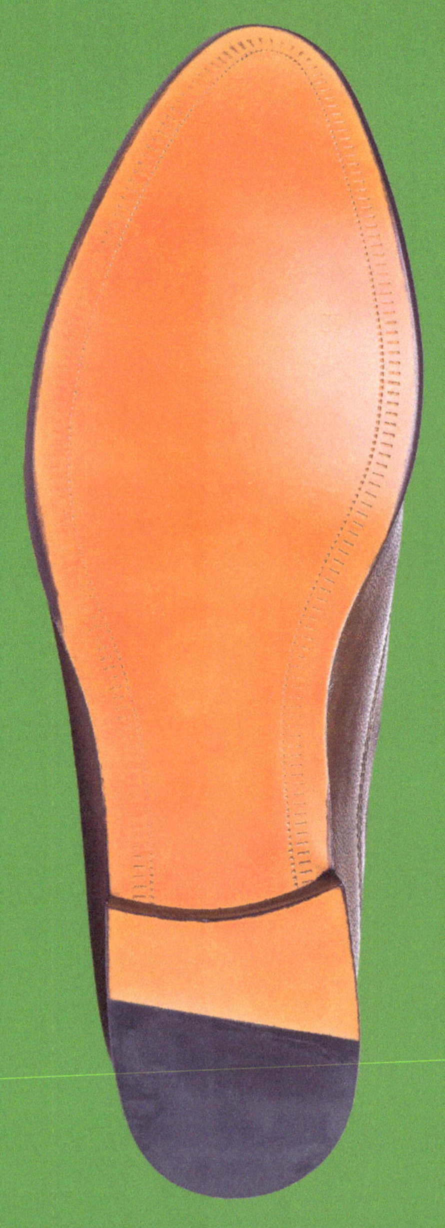

Smooth

Rough

Hard Soft

Heavy

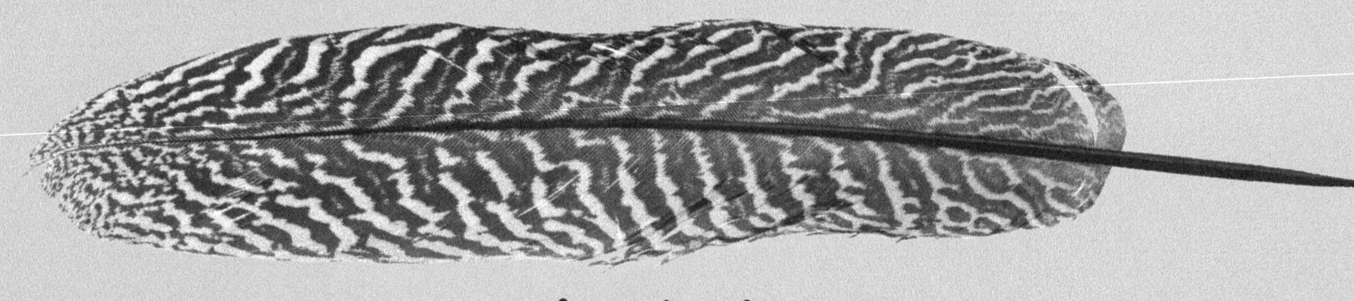

Light

Sit Stand

Above

Below

Loose

Tight

New

Old

Young

Old

On

Off

Open

Closed

Tall

Short

Near

Far

Asleep

Awake

Dark

Light

Thick

Thin

Happy

Sad

Opposites activity

Do you remember what these opposites are called? Can you find **heavy/light, in/out, hot/cold,** and **hard/soft**? Match the opposites below.

Answer: in

Answer: heavy

Answer: hot

Answer: hard

Answer: cold

Answer: soft

Answer: out

Answer: light

For other books in this series visit www.engagebooks.ca

www.ingramcontent.com/pod-product-compliance
Lightning Source LLC
LaVergne TN
LVHW070918120826
845154LV00019BB/23
9781772260762